50 Halloween Treats: Spooky and Fun Recipes

By: Kelly Johnson

Table of Contents

- Monster Cupcakes
- Witch's Potion Milkshakes
- Spider Web Brownies
- Mummy Hot Dogs
- Ghost Meringues
- Pumpkin Sugar Cookies
- Chocolate Eyeballs
- Frankenstein Rice Krispies Treats
- Witch's Broomstick Pretzels
- Candy Corn Fudge
- Graveyard Dirt Cups
- Pumpkin Patch Cupcakes
- Bat-Shaped Cookies
- Poisoned Apple Caramel Apples
- Spider Cupcakes
- Ghostly Donuts
- Frankenstein Cake Pops
- Mummy Pretzels
- Bloody Finger Cookies
- Halloween Candy Bark
- Pumpkin Pie Bites
- Monster Popcorn
- Vampire Blood Smoothie
- Skull Sugar Cookies
- Spooky Marshmallow Pops
- Witch's Cauldron Cupcakes
- Spider Web Cheesecake
- Creepy Crawly Jelly Cups
- Pumpkin Spice Cake
- Zombie Cupcakes
- Candy Corn Rice Krispies
- Witches' Fingers Cookies
- Eyeball Cake Pops
- Haunted House Brownies
- Black Cat Cupcakes

- Ghost Hot Chocolate
- Pumpkin Spice Donuts
- Candy-Coated Caramel Apples
- Witch's Potion Gummies
- Graveyard Brownie Bites
- Monster Macarons
- Spooky S'mores
- Pumpkin-Shaped Cake Pops
- Creepy Chocolate Dipped Strawberries
- Dracula's Blood Punch
- Bat-Shaped Cheesecake Bites
- Haunted Popcorn Balls
- Pumpkin Rice Krispies Treats
- Ghost Cupcakes with Marshmallow Frosting
- Spooky Chocolate Truffles

Monster Cupcakes

Ingredients:

- 1 box of chocolate cake mix
- 1 cup water
- 1/2 cup vegetable oil
- 3 large eggs
- Green food coloring
- 1 batch of buttercream frosting (recipe below)
- Candy eyes or chocolate chips for decoration

Instructions:

1. Preheat the oven to 350°F (175°C). Line a muffin tin with cupcake liners.
2. Prepare the cake mix according to the package instructions.
3. Add a few drops of green food coloring to the batter and mix until the color is uniform.
4. Pour the batter into the cupcake liners, filling them about 2/3 full.
5. Bake for 18-22 minutes, or until a toothpick inserted into the center comes out clean.
6. Allow the cupcakes to cool completely.
7. Frost with buttercream frosting and decorate with candy eyes or chocolate chips to create monster faces.

Buttercream Frosting:

- 1 cup unsalted butter, softened
- 4 cups powdered sugar
- 2 teaspoons vanilla extract
- 2 tablespoons milk
- Green food coloring

Witch's Potion Milkshakes

Ingredients:

- 2 cups vanilla ice cream
- 1 cup milk
- 2 tablespoons green food coloring
- Whipped cream (for topping)
- Candy sprinkles or green sugar (for garnish)

Instructions:

1. In a blender, combine the vanilla ice cream, milk, and green food coloring. Blend until smooth and creamy.
2. Pour the milkshake into glasses and top with whipped cream.
3. Garnish with candy sprinkles or green sugar for a magical touch.

Spider Web Brownies

Ingredients:

- 1 box of brownie mix (or homemade brownie batter)
- 1/4 cup water
- 1/2 cup vegetable oil
- 2 large eggs
- 1 cup white chocolate chips
- Black food coloring (optional)

Instructions:

1. Preheat the oven and prepare the brownie mix according to package instructions.
2. Pour the batter into a greased baking pan and bake according to the directions.
3. Let the brownies cool completely.
4. In a microwave-safe bowl, melt the white chocolate chips, adding a few drops of black food coloring if desired.
5. Once melted, drizzle the white chocolate in a spiral pattern on top of the brownies.
6. Use a toothpick to create a spider web design by gently dragging the tip from the center outward.

Mummy Hot Dogs

Ingredients:

- 1 package of hot dog sausages
- 1 package refrigerated crescent roll dough
- Mustard or ketchup (for eyes)

Instructions:

1. Preheat the oven according to the crescent roll dough package instructions.
2. Roll out the dough and cut it into thin strips.
3. Wrap the dough strips around each hot dog, leaving space for eyes.
4. Bake in the oven until the dough is golden brown, about 12-15 minutes.
5. Once baked, use mustard or ketchup to create eyes on each "mummy" hot dog.

Ghost Meringues

Ingredients:

- 4 large egg whites
- 1 cup granulated sugar
- 1/2 teaspoon vanilla extract
- Mini chocolate chips (for eyes)

Instructions:

1. Preheat the oven to 200°F (93°C) and line a baking sheet with parchment paper.
2. Beat the egg whites with a pinch of salt until soft peaks form.
3. Gradually add the sugar and beat until stiff peaks form.
4. Spoon or pipe the meringue into ghost shapes on the baking sheet.
5. Bake for 1-1.5 hours until dry and crisp.
6. Let cool, then add mini chocolate chips as eyes to complete the ghosts.

Pumpkin Sugar Cookies

Ingredients:

- 1 3/4 cups all-purpose flour
- 1 teaspoon baking powder
- 1/4 teaspoon salt
- 1/2 cup unsalted butter, softened
- 1 cup granulated sugar
- 1 large egg
- 1 teaspoon vanilla extract
- Orange food coloring
- Green sprinkles (for decoration)

Instructions:

1. Preheat the oven to 350°F (175°C) and line a baking sheet with parchment paper.
2. In a bowl, whisk together flour, baking powder, and salt.
3. In a separate bowl, beat the butter and sugar until creamy. Add the egg and vanilla extract, then mix in the dry ingredients.
4. Add orange food coloring to the dough to create a pumpkin color.
5. Roll the dough into small balls and flatten slightly on the baking sheet.
6. Bake for 10-12 minutes, until the edges are golden.
7. Once cooled, decorate with green sprinkles to resemble pumpkin vines.

Chocolate Eyeballs

Ingredients:

- 1 package chocolate truffles or large chocolate balls
- 1/2 cup white chocolate chips
- Blue or green food coloring
- Red food coloring (optional)

Instructions:

1. Melt the white chocolate chips and tint with a few drops of blue or green food coloring.
2. Dip the chocolate truffles in the colored white chocolate to make an eye.
3. Add a small drop of red food coloring to create veins if desired.
4. Place a mini chocolate chip in the center for the pupil.
5. Allow to set before serving.

Frankenstein Rice Krispies Treats

Ingredients:

- 6 cups Rice Krispies cereal
- 1 package (10 oz) marshmallows
- 3 tablespoons unsalted butter
- Green food coloring
- Black icing (for decorating)
- Candy eyes (optional)

Instructions:

1. In a large saucepan, melt the butter over low heat, then add the marshmallows and stir until completely melted.
2. Stir in a few drops of green food coloring until the mixture turns green.
3. Add the Rice Krispies cereal and mix until well coated.
4. Press the mixture into a greased 9x13-inch pan and let it cool.
5. Once cooled, cut into rectangles and decorate with black icing to create Frankenstein's facial features and add candy eyes if desired.

Witch's Broomstick Pretzels

Ingredients:

- Pretzel rods
- 1 cup semisweet chocolate chips
- 1/4 cup orange sprinkles (or candy eyes for extra fun)
- 1/2 cup candy corn (optional, for decoration)
- 1/2 cup mini marshmallows

Instructions:

1. Melt the chocolate chips in the microwave, stirring every 20 seconds until smooth.
2. Dip each pretzel rod into the melted chocolate, leaving the top uncoated to resemble the "broomstick" handle.
3. Place mini marshmallows on the uncoated end to mimic the bristles of the broom.
4. Roll the chocolate-coated pretzel in orange sprinkles or candy corn for extra Halloween flair.
5. Allow the pretzels to set by letting them cool on parchment paper.

Candy Corn Fudge

Ingredients:

- 3 cups white chocolate chips
- 1 can (14 oz) sweetened condensed milk
- 1/4 cup unsalted butter
- 1 teaspoon vanilla extract
- Yellow and orange food coloring

Instructions:

1. In a saucepan, melt the white chocolate chips, sweetened condensed milk, and butter over medium heat, stirring constantly until smooth.
2. Remove from heat and stir in the vanilla extract.
3. Divide the mixture into three bowls. Leave one bowl as is, dye the second bowl yellow, and the third orange.
4. Layer the fudge in a greased 8x8-inch pan: start with the yellow layer, then add the white layer, followed by the orange layer.
5. Let the fudge cool in the refrigerator for 2-3 hours before cutting into squares.

Graveyard Dirt Cups

Ingredients:

- 1 package chocolate pudding mix
- 2 cups milk
- 1 package Oreos, crushed
- 1 bag gummy worms
- 1/4 cup candy pumpkins or other Halloween-themed candy

Instructions:

1. Prepare the chocolate pudding according to package instructions.
2. In individual cups, layer pudding, crushed Oreos (to resemble "dirt"), and more pudding until the cups are filled.
3. Top with additional crushed Oreos, gummy worms, and candy pumpkins for a spooky graveyard effect.
4. Chill in the refrigerator for at least an hour before serving.

Pumpkin Patch Cupcakes

Ingredients:

- 1 box of vanilla cupcake mix
- 1/2 cup canned pumpkin puree
- 1 cup cinnamon and sugar mixture
- 1 batch of buttercream frosting (recipe below)
- Miniature candy pumpkins for decoration

Instructions:

1. Prepare the vanilla cupcakes according to package instructions, adding the canned pumpkin puree to the batter.
2. Bake and let the cupcakes cool completely.
3. Once cooled, frost with buttercream frosting and dip the tops into the cinnamon-sugar mixture to give them a "pumpkin patch" look.
4. Top with miniature candy pumpkins to complete the pumpkin patch.

Buttercream Frosting:

- 1 cup unsalted butter, softened
- 4 cups powdered sugar
- 2 teaspoons vanilla extract
- 2 tablespoons milk

Bat-Shaped Cookies

Ingredients:

- 1 batch of sugar cookie dough (homemade or store-bought)
- 1 batch of chocolate frosting (store-bought or homemade)
- Black food coloring
- Bat-shaped cookie cutter

Instructions:

1. Roll out the sugar cookie dough and use the bat-shaped cookie cutter to cut out bat cookies.
2. Bake according to the dough instructions and allow to cool completely.
3. Frost the cookies with chocolate frosting and decorate with black food coloring for eyes, if desired.

Poisoned Apple Caramel Apples

Ingredients:

- 6 small apples
- 1 bag caramel candies
- 2 tablespoons heavy cream
- Green food coloring
- 1 cup chopped nuts, sprinkles, or candy (optional)

Instructions:

1. Insert sticks into the apples and set aside.
2. In a saucepan, melt the caramel candies and heavy cream over low heat, stirring until smooth.
3. Add green food coloring to the caramel sauce to give it a "poisonous" hue.
4. Dip the apples into the caramel, covering them completely.
5. Roll the apples in chopped nuts or sprinkles if desired.
6. Let them set by placing them in the fridge for about 30 minutes.

Spider Cupcakes

Ingredients:

- 1 box of chocolate cake mix
- 1 batch of buttercream frosting (recipe below)
- Black licorice ropes (for spider legs)
- Candy eyes

Instructions:

1. Bake the chocolate cupcakes according to the instructions.
2. Once cooled, frost the cupcakes with a thick layer of buttercream frosting.
3. Use the black licorice ropes to create spider legs on the cupcakes.
4. Place candy eyes on top to make the spiders come to life!

Buttercream Frosting:

- 1 cup unsalted butter, softened
- 4 cups powdered sugar
- 2 teaspoons vanilla extract
- 2 tablespoons milk

Ghostly Donuts

Ingredients:

- 1 package of powdered donuts
- 1/4 cup white chocolate chips
- 1/4 cup mini marshmallows
- Black icing (for eyes)

Instructions:

1. Melt the white chocolate chips in the microwave, stirring every 20 seconds until smooth.
2. Dip the powdered donuts into the melted white chocolate to cover the top.
3. While the chocolate is still soft, place two mini marshmallows at the top of the donut to form the ghost's "head."
4. Use black icing to pipe eyes and a mouth onto each marshmallow.
5. Allow the donuts to cool and set before serving.

Frankenstein Cake Pops

Ingredients:

- 1 box of chocolate cake mix
- 1 batch of chocolate frosting
- Green candy melts
- Black icing for details (eyes, mouth, bolts)
- Lollipop sticks

Instructions:

1. Bake the chocolate cake according to the package instructions and let it cool.
2. Crumble the cake into a large bowl and mix with chocolate frosting until it forms a dough-like consistency.
3. Shape the mixture into small balls and insert a lollipop stick into each.
4. Dip each cake pop into the green candy melts, covering it entirely.
5. Use black icing to pipe Frankenstein's features, such as eyes, a mouth, and bolts on the sides of his neck.
6. Let the cake pops set before serving.

Mummy Pretzels

Ingredients:

- Pretzel rods
- 1 cup white chocolate chips
- Candy eyes
- Black icing (optional)

Instructions:

1. Melt the white chocolate chips in the microwave, stirring every 20 seconds until smooth.
2. Dip each pretzel rod into the white chocolate, leaving a small part at the top uncovered.
3. Lay the chocolate-dipped pretzels on wax paper and drizzle more white chocolate over the pretzels in a crisscross pattern to resemble mummy wrappings.
4. Place candy eyes on the top of each pretzel to create a mummy face.
5. Allow the chocolate to set before serving.

Bloody Finger Cookies

Ingredients:

- 1 batch of sugar cookie dough
- 1/4 cup sliced almonds (for fingernails)
- Red food gel (for blood)

Instructions:

1. Roll out the sugar cookie dough and cut into long, thin shapes to resemble fingers.
2. Use the sliced almonds to create fingernails by pressing them at the tip of each cookie.
3. Place the "fingers" on a baking sheet and bake according to the dough instructions.
4. Once cooled, use red food gel to create a bloody effect at the base of each finger.
5. Serve these eerie treats with a side of spooky "blood" (a red raspberry syrup or similar).

Halloween Candy Bark

Ingredients:

- 1 bag of dark chocolate chips
- 1 bag of white chocolate chips
- Halloween candy (candy corn, mini marshmallows, gummy worms, etc.)
- Sprinkles (optional)

Instructions:

1. Melt the dark chocolate and white chocolate chips in separate bowls, stirring until smooth.
2. Spread the dark chocolate evenly on a parchment-lined baking sheet, then drizzle the white chocolate over the top in a swirling pattern.
3. Sprinkle the Halloween candy and sprinkles over the bark while the chocolate is still soft.
4. Let the bark cool in the fridge for at least an hour before breaking it into pieces.

Pumpkin Pie Bites

Ingredients:

- 1 package refrigerated pie crusts
- 1 can pumpkin puree
- 1/2 cup sweetened condensed milk
- 1 teaspoon cinnamon
- 1/2 teaspoon nutmeg
- 1 egg

Instructions:

1. Preheat the oven to 375°F (190°C).
2. Roll out the pie crusts and cut them into small circles using a cookie cutter or a glass.
3. In a bowl, mix together the pumpkin puree, sweetened condensed milk, cinnamon, nutmeg, and egg until smooth.
4. Place a spoonful of the pumpkin mixture onto each pie crust circle, then fold the edges over slightly to create little hand pies.
5. Bake the pies on a baking sheet for 15-20 minutes, or until golden brown.
6. Let them cool before serving.

Monster Popcorn

Ingredients:

- 1 bag of microwave popcorn
- 1/2 cup green candy melts
- 1/2 cup purple candy melts
- Candy eyes
- Halloween sprinkles

Instructions:

1. Pop the popcorn and spread it out on a parchment-lined baking sheet.
2. Melt the green and purple candy melts separately, stirring until smooth.
3. Drizzle the melted candy over the popcorn, creating a colorful monster-like appearance.
4. Add candy eyes and Halloween sprinkles for extra spooky flair.
5. Let the popcorn cool and harden before serving.

Vampire Blood Smoothie

Ingredients:

- 1 cup frozen strawberries
- 1/2 cup pomegranate juice
- 1/2 cup coconut milk
- 1 tablespoon honey (optional)
- Red food coloring (optional)

Instructions:

1. Blend together the frozen strawberries, pomegranate juice, coconut milk, and honey until smooth.
2. Add a few drops of red food coloring for extra "blood" effect if desired.
3. Pour the smoothie into glasses and serve with a straw or a spooky garnish like a plastic spider.

Skull Sugar Cookies

Ingredients:

- 1 batch of sugar cookie dough
- Skull-shaped cookie cutter
- Royal icing (recipe below)
- Black and white food coloring

Instructions:

1. Roll out the sugar cookie dough and cut into skull shapes using the skull cookie cutter.
2. Bake according to the dough instructions and let cool.
3. Use royal icing to decorate the skulls with spooky details like eyes, noses, and teeth.
4. Let the icing set before serving.

Royal Icing:

- 2 cups powdered sugar
- 2 tablespoons meringue powder
- 1/4 cup water
- 1 teaspoon vanilla extract

Spooky Marshmallow Pops

Ingredients:

- 1 bag of large marshmallows
- 1 cup white chocolate chips
- Halloween sprinkles (optional)
- Lollipop sticks
- Black food coloring

Instructions:

1. Insert a lollipop stick into each marshmallow.
2. Melt the white chocolate chips in the microwave, stirring every 20 seconds until smooth.
3. Dip each marshmallow into the melted chocolate and add Halloween sprinkles for a festive touch.
4. Use black food coloring to pipe spooky designs or faces on each marshmallow pop.
5. Let the chocolate set before serving.

Witch's Cauldron Cupcakes

Ingredients:

- 1 box of chocolate cake mix
- 1 batch of chocolate buttercream frosting
- Green food coloring
- Candy eyes
- Black licorice (for the cauldron handle)

Instructions:

1. Bake the chocolate cupcakes according to the package instructions and let them cool completely.
2. Dye the buttercream frosting green with food coloring and frost the cupcakes.
3. Use black licorice to create handles on the side of the cupcakes to mimic a cauldron.
4. Place candy eyes on top to add a creepy touch.
5. Optional: Decorate with edible glitter or candy to make it look like bubbling potion.

Spider Web Cheesecake

Ingredients:

- 1 graham cracker crust
- 3 packages cream cheese
- 1 cup sour cream
- 1/2 cup sugar
- 3 eggs
- 1 teaspoon vanilla
- 1/4 cup chocolate syrup
- 1/4 cup heavy cream

Instructions:

1. Preheat the oven to 325°F (160°C).
2. Beat together the cream cheese, sour cream, sugar, eggs, and vanilla until smooth.
3. Pour the mixture into the graham cracker crust and bake for 50-60 minutes.
4. Let the cheesecake cool completely.
5. Use chocolate syrup to draw a spider web design on the top of the cheesecake.
6. Gently swirl the chocolate syrup with a toothpick to create a web effect.

Creepy Crawly Jelly Cups

Ingredients:

- 1 packet of black cherry or blackberry jelly
- Gummy worms
- Plastic cups

Instructions:

1. Prepare the jelly according to the packet instructions and pour into small plastic cups.
2. Drop a few gummy worms into the cups before the jelly sets.
3. Refrigerate until the jelly is firm.
4. For added spookiness, you can also add fake bugs or eyeballs to the jelly cups.

Pumpkin Spice Cake

Ingredients:

- 1 box of yellow cake mix
- 1 can of pumpkin puree
- 1 tablespoon pumpkin spice
- 1 teaspoon cinnamon
- 1 batch of cream cheese frosting

Instructions:

1. Preheat the oven to 350°F (175°C).
2. Mix the cake mix, pumpkin puree, pumpkin spice, and cinnamon until well combined.
3. Pour into a greased cake pan and bake according to the package instructions.
4. Let the cake cool and then frost with cream cheese frosting.
5. Optional: Garnish with candy pumpkins or sprinkle cinnamon on top for added effect.

Zombie Cupcakes

Ingredients:

- 1 box of vanilla cake mix
- 1 batch of green frosting
- Red gel food coloring
- Candy eyes
- Chocolate sprinkles

Instructions:

1. Bake the vanilla cupcakes according to the package instructions and let cool.
2. Frost each cupcake with green frosting.
3. Use red gel food coloring to create blood drips around the edges of the cupcakes.
4. Place candy eyes on top of each cupcake.
5. Add chocolate sprinkles for texture to resemble "zombie" dirt.

Candy Corn Rice Krispies

Ingredients:

- 1 box of Rice Krispies cereal
- 3 tablespoons butter
- 1 bag of marshmallows
- Yellow and orange food coloring

Instructions:

1. Melt the butter and marshmallows in a large pot.
2. Mix in the Rice Krispies cereal and stir until fully combined.
3. Divide the mixture into three bowls.
4. Dye one bowl yellow, one orange, and leave the third one white.
5. Layer the colored mixtures in a baking pan to create a candy corn effect.
6. Let cool and cut into squares.

Witches' Fingers Cookies

Ingredients:

- 1 package of sugar cookie dough
- Sliced almonds (for fingernails)
- Green food coloring

Instructions:

1. Preheat the oven to 350°F (175°C).
2. Roll the cookie dough into long, finger-like shapes.
3. Press a sliced almond onto the tip of each cookie to resemble a fingernail.
4. Bake according to the package instructions.
5. After baking, paint the tips of the "fingers" with green food coloring for an eerie effect.

Eyeball Cake Pops

Ingredients:

- 1 box of vanilla cake mix
- 1 batch of vanilla frosting
- White candy melts
- Red food coloring
- Candy eyes

Instructions:

1. Bake the vanilla cake according to the package instructions and let it cool.
2. Crumble the cake into small pieces and mix with the vanilla frosting until it forms a dough-like consistency.
3. Roll the mixture into balls and place a lollipop stick in each one.
4. Dip each cake pop into the white candy melts and allow the coating to harden.
5. Use red food coloring to draw veins on the cake pops for a creepy eyeball effect.
6. Add candy eyes in the center of each cake pop to complete the look.

Haunted House Brownies

Ingredients:

- 1 box of brownie mix (or your favorite homemade recipe)
- 1 batch of chocolate ganache or frosting
- Halloween-themed candies (such as gummy worms, candy eyeballs, and mini chocolate bars)
- Black and orange sprinkles

Instructions:

1. Prepare the brownies according to the package or your homemade recipe instructions and bake them.
2. Once cooled, cut the brownies into squares.
3. Frost the brownies with chocolate ganache or frosting to create a "house" shape.
4. Decorate with Halloween candies, such as gummy worms for creepy critters or candy eyeballs to add a haunted vibe.
5. Sprinkle with black and orange sprinkles for an extra spooky touch.

Black Cat Cupcakes

Ingredients:

- 1 box of chocolate cake mix (or your favorite chocolate cupcake recipe)
- 1 batch of black buttercream frosting
- Yellow fondant or candy (for the eyes)
- Black licorice (for the tail)
- Chocolate chips (for the nose)

Instructions:

1. Bake the chocolate cupcakes and let them cool.
2. Frost each cupcake with black buttercream frosting.
3. Use yellow fondant or candy to make eyes and place them on the cupcakes.
4. Shape black licorice into tails and place them on the cupcakes.
5. Add chocolate chips as noses to complete the look of the black cat.

Ghost Hot Chocolate

Ingredients:

- 2 cups of milk
- 1/2 cup of heavy cream
- 1/2 cup of cocoa powder
- 1/2 cup of sugar
- 1/4 teaspoon of vanilla extract
- Mini marshmallows
- Dark chocolate chips (for eyes)

Instructions:

1. Heat the milk and heavy cream in a saucepan over medium heat until warm.
2. Whisk in the cocoa powder, sugar, and vanilla extract until smooth.
3. Pour the hot chocolate into mugs.
4. Use mini marshmallows to form ghost shapes on top of the hot chocolate, and then add dark chocolate chips for eyes.
5. Serve hot and enjoy the spooky warmth!

Pumpkin Spice Donuts

Ingredients:

- 1 box of cake mix (or your favorite donut recipe)
- 1 can of pumpkin puree
- 1 teaspoon of pumpkin pie spice
- 1/2 teaspoon cinnamon
- Powdered sugar or cinnamon sugar for coating

Instructions:

1. Preheat the oven to 350°F (175°C).
2. In a bowl, combine the cake mix, pumpkin puree, pumpkin pie spice, and cinnamon.
3. Spoon the mixture into a donut pan, filling each well about 2/3 full.
4. Bake for 12-15 minutes or until a toothpick comes out clean.
5. Once the donuts have cooled slightly, roll them in powdered sugar or cinnamon sugar.

Candy-Coated Caramel Apples

Ingredients:

- 6 apples
- 1 bag of caramel squares
- 1 tablespoon of heavy cream
- 1 cup of Halloween candy (chopped Snickers, M&Ms, crushed Oreos, etc.)

Instructions:

1. Stick a wooden stick into the top of each apple.
2. Melt the caramel and heavy cream together in a saucepan over low heat, stirring constantly until smooth.
3. Dip each apple into the caramel mixture, coating it evenly.
4. Roll the caramel-coated apples in chopped Halloween candy.
5. Allow the caramel to set before serving.

Witch's Potion Gummies

Ingredients:

- 1 package of lime Jell-O
- 1 package of orange Jell-O
- 1 package of gelatin (unflavored)
- 1/2 cup of boiling water
- Halloween gummy candies (eyeballs, worms, etc.)

Instructions:

1. Dissolve the lime Jell-O and unflavored gelatin in 1/4 cup of boiling water, then pour into gummy molds.
2. Let the lime mixture set in the refrigerator for 1-2 hours.
3. Repeat with the orange Jell-O and pour it over the lime layer.
4. Allow the entire mold to set for another 2-3 hours.
5. Once firm, remove from the molds and decorate with Halloween gummy candies for a spooky effect.

Graveyard Brownie Bites

Ingredients:

- 1 batch of brownies (homemade or box mix)
- 1 batch of chocolate frosting
- Mini chocolate cookies (for tombstones)
- Candy bones or ghosts

Instructions:

1. Prepare the brownies and cut them into bite-sized squares.
2. Frost each brownie with a layer of chocolate frosting.
3. Stick mini chocolate cookies into the frosting to resemble tombstones.
4. Add candy bones or ghosts on top for a creepy graveyard look.

Monster Macarons

Ingredients:

- 1 batch of macaron shells (made with almond flour, egg whites, powdered sugar)
- Green buttercream frosting
- Candy eyes
- Chocolate chips for decoration

Instructions:

1. Prepare and bake the macaron shells according to your favorite macaron recipe.
2. Once the shells have cooled, pipe green buttercream frosting onto one half of each macaron.
3. Sandwich the macarons together.
4. Decorate the top with candy eyes and chocolate chips to make your macarons look like silly, spooky monsters.

Spooky S'mores

Ingredients:

- Graham crackers
- Marshmallows
- Dark chocolate (or Halloween-themed chocolate bars)
- Orange and black sprinkles for decoration

Instructions:

1. Break the graham crackers into squares.
2. Toast the marshmallows until golden and gooey.
3. Place a piece of dark chocolate on one graham cracker square, followed by the toasted marshmallow.
4. Top with another graham cracker to form the s'more.
5. For a spooky twist, sprinkle the edges with orange and black sprinkles.

Pumpkin-Shaped Cake Pops

Ingredients:

- 1 batch of your favorite cake (vanilla, pumpkin, or chocolate)
- 1 batch of frosting
- Orange candy melts
- Green candy (for leaves and stems)

Instructions:

1. Bake the cake and crumble it into fine crumbs.
2. Mix the cake crumbs with frosting until it forms a dough-like consistency.
3. Roll the mixture into small balls and insert cake pop sticks.
4. Dip the cake pops in melted orange candy melts to coat them.
5. Once the candy has set, add green candy for leaves and stems to complete the pumpkin shape.

Creepy Chocolate Dipped Strawberries

Ingredients:

- Fresh strawberries
- Dark chocolate or white chocolate
- Red food coloring (for blood effect)
- Halloween sprinkles or edible glitter

Instructions:

1. Melt the chocolate and dip each strawberry in the melted chocolate, coating it completely.
2. Drizzle a bit of red food coloring over the chocolate-covered strawberries to create a "blood" effect.
3. Decorate with Halloween sprinkles or edible glitter for an eerie look.
4. Let them set in the fridge before serving.

Dracula's Blood Punch

Ingredients:

- 1 liter of cranberry juice
- 2 cups of orange juice
- 1 cup of lemon-lime soda
- Red food coloring (optional)
- Ice cubes (frozen with gummy worms inside)
- Red fruit (such as strawberries or raspberries) for garnish

Instructions:

1. In a large punch bowl, combine cranberry juice, orange juice, and lemon-lime soda.
2. Add a few drops of red food coloring for an extra "bloody" look.
3. Freeze gummy worms inside ice cubes and add them to the punch for a creepy twist.
4. Garnish with fresh red fruit and serve chilled.

Bat-Shaped Cheesecake Bites

Ingredients:

- Mini cheesecakes (store-bought or homemade)
- Black fondant or black decorating gel
- Candy eyes

Instructions:

1. Prepare mini cheesecakes and let them cool.
2. Roll out black fondant and cut it into bat shapes using a bat-shaped cookie cutter or freehand.
3. Place the bat shapes on top of each cheesecake bite.
4. Add candy eyes to the bats to make them look extra spooky.

Haunted Popcorn Balls

Ingredients:

- 1 bag of popcorn (popped)
- 1/2 cup of butter
- 1/2 cup of sugar
- 1/2 cup of corn syrup
- 1/2 teaspoon of vanilla extract
- Halloween candy for decoration (candy corn, mini chocolate bars, or sprinkles)

Instructions:

1. Melt the butter, sugar, and corn syrup in a saucepan over medium heat until combined.
2. Stir in the vanilla extract.
3. Pour the mixture over the popped popcorn and stir until well-coated.
4. Allow the mixture to cool slightly, then form into balls.
5. Decorate with Halloween candies for a spooky touch.

Pumpkin Rice Krispies Treats

Ingredients:

- 6 cups of Rice Krispies cereal
- 1 bag of marshmallows
- 3 tablespoons of butter
- Orange food coloring
- Green licorice (for pumpkin stems)

Instructions:

1. Melt the butter and marshmallows together in a large saucepan.
2. Stir in orange food coloring until the mixture turns a pumpkin orange.
3. Mix in the Rice Krispies until well-coated.
4. Press the mixture into a greased pan and let it set.
5. Once cooled, cut the treats into pumpkin shapes and decorate with green licorice for the stems.

Ghost Cupcakes with Marshmallow Frosting

Ingredients:

- 1 batch of your favorite cupcake batter (vanilla, chocolate, or pumpkin)
- 1 batch of marshmallow frosting
- Black food coloring or black gel (for eyes)

Instructions:

1. Bake the cupcakes according to the recipe instructions and let them cool.
2. Frost each cupcake with fluffy marshmallow frosting.
3. Use black food coloring or gel to create spooky eyes and mouth shapes on the frosting.
4. Serve the ghostly cupcakes at your Halloween party.

Spooky Chocolate Truffles

Ingredients:

- 8 oz of dark or milk chocolate
- 1/2 cup of heavy cream
- Halloween sprinkles or cocoa powder for coating

Instructions:

1. Heat the cream in a saucepan until just simmering, then pour it over the chopped chocolate.
2. Stir until the chocolate is completely melted and smooth.
3. Let the mixture cool in the fridge for 2 hours until firm.
4. Scoop out the mixture and roll it into small balls.
5. Roll the truffles in Halloween sprinkles or cocoa powder for a spooky finish.